Ollie the Octopus

Story and Pictures by
Betty L. Duncan

Order this book online at www.trafford.com
or email orders@trafford.com

Most Trafford titles are also available at major online book retailers.

www.trafford.com

North America & international
toll-free: 844-688-6899 (USA & Canada)
fax: 812 355 4082

Our mission is to efficiently provide the world's finest, most comprehensive book publishing service, enabling every author to experience success. To find out how to publish your book, your way, and have it available worldwide, visit us online at www.trafford.com

ISBN: 978-1-4251-0089-6

Print information available on the last page.

Trafford rev.09/27/2019

To My Grandchildren
Luke & Laura

Ollie Octopus and Freddie Fish were friends.

Sometimes Ollie would put her long arms around Freddie.

One day Freddie swam
away all by himself.
He left Ollie at home –
asleep.

Ollie was very, very sleepy.
She slept and slept.

When Ollie woke up she looked all around for her friend Freddie.

"Where is my little
friend Freddie?"
she asked Sammy Starfish.
But Sammy Starfish
did not know.

"Where is my friend Freddie?"
She asked Mr. Crab.
Mr. Crab shook his pincers and scurried away beneath the sand.

Swordfish shook his long,
long sharp snout.
He had not seen Freddie!

Mr. Elmer Eel had not seen Freddie, and he said so as he wiggled his long green tail.

Just then Ollie
saw something strange
in the water!

Then Ollie saw her friend Freddie—and Freddie was about to swallow the strange thing!

“STOP!
Don’t swallow that!”
said Ollie.

“Why not?”
said Freddie,
“I’m hungry!”

"Come with me,"
said Ollie.
"I'll find you some
safe food."

"O.K," said Freddie.
So Ollie and her
friend swam away...

together.

OLLIE THE OCTOPUS

Words and Music by Betty L. Duncan

Reader's Note

Ollie Octopus and Freddie Fish are friends in the undersea world created by this author. Ollie is a good friend and saves Freddie from disaster. Freddie learns that not all things that look good are indeed good for him. He learns a valuable lesson and he and Ollie swim away together. Listen closely to hear the little song they sing together in this delightful story of undersea adventures.

For children ages 4 to 7.

Printed in the United States
by Baker & Taylor Publisher Services